World Trivia

*The book of fascinating facts:
culture, politics and geography*

By Michael Smith

Cover art illustration by Crystal Smith
Book illustrations by Cash Donovan
Book design by Albert Lin (Apococo Visual Image)

Second Edition

East West Discovery Press

Published by:
East West Discovery Press
P.O. Box 2393, Gardena, CA 90247
Phone: 310-532-1115, Fax: 310-768-8926

Editor: Gillian Dale
Cover art illustration by Crystal Smith
Book illustrations by Cash Donovan
Book design by Albert Lin (Apococo Visual Image)
Maps created from the CIA web site.

First edition, 2000
Second edition, 2003 (Revised)
Printed in Canada. Published in the United States of America

Publisher's Cataloging-in-Publication
(Provided by Quality Books, Inc.)

Smith, Michael, 1961-
    World trivia: the book of fascinating facts :
  culture, politics and geography / by Michael Smith ;
  illustrator, Cash Donovan ; cover art by Crystal Smith.
  -- 2nd ed.
    p. cm.
    LCCN 2002094729
    ISBN 0-9669437-2-4

    1. Questions and answers. 2. Geography--Miscellanea.
3. Political science--Miscellanea. I. Title.

AG195.S555 2003   031.02
                         QBI02-200704

LCCN: 2002094729
ISBN: 0-9669437-2-4

Books may be purchased in bulk or customized for promotional or educational purposes.
Inquiries for foreign language translation, distribution, rights and permissions should be
addressed to: East West Discovery Press, P.O. Box 2393, Gardena, CA 90247.

Special Thanks

I wish to thank my former professor, Gillian Dale, who taught me I could write, and who more recently edited this book. I also want to thank my daughter Crystal for the cover illustration and my wife for her loving support and wisdom.

Responses to this book:

Though the material in the book has been extensively researched, facts can become obsolete and mistakes can be made. I would appreciate comments, corrections and feedback. You may contact the author by email to wittymike@hotmail.com.

What country has almost no native plant life ?

1

a.

Qatar. This desolate
peninsular country on the
Persian Gulf has managed
to "green" itself only
slightly with its oil revenue.

SAUDI
ARABIA

UNITED ARAB
EMIRATES

One fifth of all Africans live in what country ?

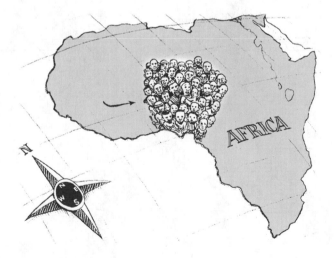

3

a.

Nigeria, with a population greater than 100 million and growing.

Which is the only Asian country never to have been occupied by a foreign power ?

a.

Thailand. The rest of East Asia has a long history of changing occupations. The USSR was both occupied and occupier: they were invaded by both Napoleon's and Hitler's army, but later controlled much of central Asia. Much of China's coast has also been under foreign domination, but now Tibet is under its rule. Holland colonized Indonesia; France controlled Laos, Cambodia and Vietnam; Spain ran the Philippines; and Britain dominated a huge area, from the Middle East to the Indian subcontinent and beyond. Japan was one of the last of the occupiers, starting with Korea and China and making its way down to South East Asia before being pushed back at the end of WWII. It was then, in turn, under U.S. occupation following the war.

In which European country do women dress in black for years following the death of a relative ?

Greece. A woman will usually wear black for three years after the death of a husband and one year following the death of another immediate family member. When the years are added together, an elderly woman may wear black until the end of her life.

Q.

In which country is marriage often entered into by couples only after many years of living together?

a.

Sweden and other parts of northern Europe. Postponing marriage is becoming the norm. Most children are born outside of marriage but are well taken care of. At a later date, marriage can act to reaffirm the longtime relationship.

Q.

**Which countries have time zones
that are a half-hour off the rest of the world?**

*Afghanistan, India, Iran,
Sri Lanka and parts of
Canada and Australia.*

Political Map of the World, April 2001

Which country has the highest percentage of
its population incarcerated ?

a.

The United States.
More than four people per
every 1000 are in jail; South
Africa is a close second.

*Which two capital cites in Africa have
names similar to the names of
their respective countries ?*

a.

*Tunis, Tunisia and
Algiers, Algeria.*

Q.

*What country has laws providing
for the public beating of a woman unfaithful
to her husband ?*

a.

The Sudan. For such crimes women can even be stoned to death under their strict interpretation of Islamic law. Afghanistan has relaxed similar laws recently with the end of Taliban rule. Regions of other countries follow similar traditions even when not sanctioned by the government.

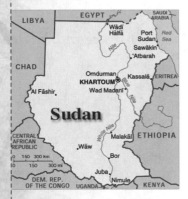

Q.

Where in 1994, was looting so bad that even many street pipes were pulled out of the ground and sold as scrap metal ?

a.

Mogadishu, Somalia. The anarchy caused some areas to be literally stripped of any material value.

DJIBOUTI   Gulf of Aden

Somalia

MOGADISHU ⊛

Indian
Ocean

KENYA

0   150   300 km
0   150   300 mi

Which continent has only one river ?

Antarctica. The sole river on the mostly frozen landmass flows only in the summer.

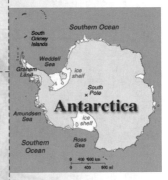

Q.

Which country is led by a man whose title is simply "Leader", who has an all female crew of bodyguards and conducts much of the country's affairs from a tent ?

a.

Libya. Muammar Gadhafi has a relatively progressive attitude on women's rights, symbolized by the female bodyguards.

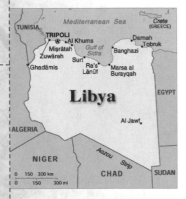

24

Q.

In which African country are the original people of Malay-Polynesian ancestry ?

Madagascar. Much later these natives mixed with freed black slaves and others, forming the present population.

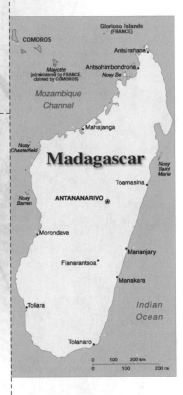

Which Asian country's government is administered mostly by people of Malay descent, while its business is performed mostly by Chinese, and its labor accomplished most often by people of Indian and Bangladeshi heritage ?

a.

Malaysia.

Where did the Japanese launch a full-scale invasion the day after the bombing of Pearl Harbor ?

a.

The former British colony of Hong Kong. Until December 8, 1941, Hong Kong had played a crucial role as an arms supply channel in China's war effort against the Japanese.

Where is it considered rude to show
the bottom of one's feet ?

In several countries, but it may be considered the most offensive in Thailand. When dignitaries are to travel under a bridge, the bridge is sometimes cleared of people, to prevent the dignitaries from being disrespected by being under the bottoms of anyone's feet.

Which two cities share their names with a popular breed of dog?

a.

Chihuahua and Labrador. Chihuahua in North Mexico has few if any of the breed, but Labrador Retrievers are common in Labrador City, Newfoundland, Canada.

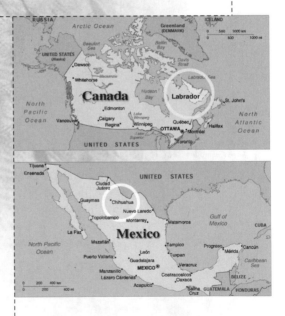

Of the world's tallest waterfalls, five out of ten are in which country ?

35

a.

Norway.

Angel Falls, Venezuela	*3,212 fts.*
Tugela Falls, South Africa	*3,110 fts.*
Utigordsfossen, Norway	*2,625 fts.*
Mongefossen, Norway	*2,540 fts.*
Yosemite Falls, USA	*2,425 fts.*
Espelandsfoss, Norway	*2,307 fts.*
Qstre Mardalsfossen, Norway	*2,149 fts.*
Cuquenan Falls, Venezuela	*2,000 fts.*
Mardalsfoss Falls, Norway	*2,000 fts.*
Sentinel Falls, USA	*2,000 fts.*

In which Asian country do most rural people live in camel skin or felt cloth houses ?

a.

Mongolia. These houses are called yurts and gers.

In which country are more than half of
all pregnancies terminated ?

39

a.

Russia. Though the practice has declined somewhat, abortion is still the only form of birth control used by millions of woman.

*Which country has the largest population of
North Koreans outside of North Korea ?*

Japan. Money sent home by Koreans in Japan provides an important economic boost to North Korea. Many Koreans in Japan have had business success, some owning Pachinko (pinball gambling) parlors.

Which country has the most nuclear reactors ?

a.

The USA has about 111 major reactors, more than twice as many as any other country.

44

Q.

Which city has such bad air pollution that just living there, one study said, is like smoking 20 cigarettes a day?

*a.*

Delhi, India. Air pollution has been similarly dangerous in other cities including Mumbai, Manila, Bangkok, Mexico City and several cities in China.

Q.

In which major city are goldfish tanks found in the front lobby of almost every office?

a.

Hong Kong. According to the practice of Feng-shui, the careful arrangement of furniture and other items in or around a building or other space can help insure success. Goldfish are believed to scare off evil spirits.

CHINA

Hong Kong

Hau Hoi Wan

Tai Pang Wan

Lantau Island

Kowloon

Hong Kong

Aberdeen

Hong Kong Island

South China Sea

*Which country's national sport is
a competitive game between men on horses
trying to drag a headless calf's carcass
around an arena ?*

49

Afghanistan. There are two different types of Buzkashi: Tudabari, and the more complicated Qarajai. Both are professional sports requiring years of training by both player and horse. Injuries such as broken arms are common. Winners may receive fancy clothing, turbans or money.

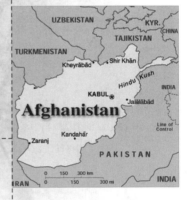

Q.

Which country uses both the French franc and the Spanish peseta ?

a.

Andorra, a small country
bordering France and
Spain.

The majority of people in Japan feel culturally related, most closely, to people in which country ?

a.

The USA. Though many Japanese feel themselves especially unique, they have borrowed much from other cultures. American culture in particular has had a phenomenal influence on modern Japanese people.

*In which country is collecting mushrooms
a major national hobby ?*

a.

Russia. Mushrooming on summer vacation in Siberia is very popular.

56

Q.

Before Germany became a country, what was the name of the region ?

a.

The Holy Roman Empire.
Ironically, it was neither
holy, Roman nor an
empire; instead it was a
collection of fragmented
independent regions and
city-states. Germany is a
relatively young country,
not unified until the late
1800's.

58

Former member states of the USSR are now united under which name ?

a.

The CIS. The Commonwealth of Independent States is an organization formed for trade cooperation.

In which country did Buddhism originate ?

a.

India. Now less popular in India, it is the most common religion in East Asia.

Which country is part of the United Kingdom but not of Great Britain ?

Northern Ireland.

The geography of which Middle Eastern country is the most comparable to California — with mild climate, beautiful beaches and snowcapped mountains ?

Lebanon. Modern Lebanon may seem out of place in the Middle East. It not only has an idyllic climate, it also has mountain ski resorts, an especially diverse religious mixture, and a capital, Beirut which feels more European than Middle Eastern.

Q.

*What South American city was said to have had
a mountain of nearly solid silver ?*

a.

Potosi, Bolivia. At the height of the mining period in the 1600's, it was the largest city in the Americas, with the third largest population in the world, built by the wealth from tons of silver mined nearby.

Which Asian country has the highest percentage of Catholics ?

a.

The Philippines is over 83% Catholic. Protestants and Moslems form the largest two minority groups.

Q.

What was the bikini named after ?

a.

The Bikini Atolls of the South Pacific.

Q.

*Which Central American country uses English
as the official language ?*

a.

Belize, formerly a British colony.

Where were over a million people executed solely for such "crimes" as being members of the middle class, having foreign friends, knowing a foreign language, or even for wearing glasses ?

75

a.

*Cambodia. In 1975, the
Khmer Rouge committed
genocide against its own
people, attempting to rid the
country of all who were not
simple peasants.*

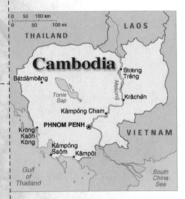

In the former Soviet Union what was the most common second language spoken ?

a.

Russian. Learning their local language at home, more people spoke Russian as a second language than as a first.

Simon Bolivar tried to unite which countries ?

a.

Venezuela, Colombia, Panama, Equador, and his namesake, Bolivia. However, he failed to create the country that he wanted, Grand Columbia.

Q.

In which country are over 99% of all females circumcised ?

a.

Djibouti, North Africa. Various forms of female genital mutilation exist in Africa, the Middle East and other locations. At least 90 million girls worldwide are affected, in more than 30 countries. Female circumcision can range from a slight incision, to removal of the clitoris and sewing up the vagina. Both male and female circumcision are normally medically unnecessary and both increasingly being questioned.

Which country has only one main written language but about 35 spoken languages ?

a.

China.

Which Asian country has four written languages but only one spoken language ?

a.

Japan has Kanji, characters similar to Chinese; Hiragana, a syllabic alphabet; Katakana, used to pronounce foreign words; and Romanji, using western letters.

Q.

Which country has more than 500 religious cults that require the donation of all of the follower's money?

a.

The United States.

*Which U.S. states are farthest south ?
north ? west ? east ?*

*Hawaii is the most south;
Alaska the most north, the
most west, and as it crosses
the 180° longitude line, the
most east.*

Which country has no government ?

a.

Somalia, which is run by various armed gangs.

Q.

*Which Central American country has had
a U.S. citizen as its president?*

a.

At one time, Nicaragua's president was William Walker, the conqueror from Tennessee. In the 1850's his private army also occupied parts of Baja California before his demise.

Q.

Which European country, in modern history, "sold" about 33,000 of its citizens to a neighboring country ?

a.

East Germany. From the 1960's through 1980's, it profited greatly by charging high fees to West Germany, which was trying to buy freedom for political prisoners.

Which country requires a government escort for foreign visitors ?

97

a.

North Korea, where visitors' actions are monitored carefully. Though very different from North Korea, Bhutan also has regulations that limit independent travel. They require guides, and travelers must pay a fee of more than $200 a day.

Which country has two cooperative federal governmental systems, both currently in practice ?

a.

China. In the 1997 reversion of Hong Kong to China, a "one country/two systems" government was created.

**Which Latin American country does not
have its own currency ?**

a.

Panama, which uses the
U.S. dollar, is also known as
a place where money is
laundered.

In what region would you use the currencies of the Kip, Dong, Baht, Riel and Kyat ?

*In South East Asia. They
are, in order, from Laos,
Vietnam, Thailand,
Cambodia and Myanmar.*

As a foreign visitor where would one have to use
a currency different than local residents ?

a.

In Myanmar. The Kyats is the normal currency. Tourists are supposed to use a special tourist currency called the FEC. China previously had a similar system. Interestingly, Myanmar's currency is printed in China.

Where in the United States is marriage, without the consent of the parents, legal only at 21 years of age and above ?

a.

Puerto Rico.

In which country do women sometimes have more than one husband (not the other way around)?

a.

Nepal. This unique kind of polygamy happens when the prospective husbands pool their resources to afford the high cost of a dowry.

What country has 17,508 islands ?

a.

Indonesia, with the most islands of any country.

Of the countries that do not have a criminal extradition treaty with the United States, which is geographically closest?

a.

Brazil. A good number of *fugitives from the United States are resident there.*

What is the only U.S. state to border only one other state ?

a.

Maine. It is also the only state with a monosyllabic name.

In which East Asian city do all citizens
have the right to reside in Europe ?

a.

Macau, a former Portuguese colony on China's southern coast, which has reverted back to China's sovereignty. Unlike Britain in its treatment of citizens of Hong Kong, Portugal has offered any citizen of Macau the right to live in the home country.

CHINA

Macau

Macau

Zhujiang Kou

breakwater

government house

bridge

bridge

taxiway

Ilha da Taipa

Taipa

airport

causeway

taxiway

Xiaohengqin Dao

CHINA

Coloane

Ilha de Coloane

Dahengqin Dao

South China Sea

0   1 km   2 km

0   1   2 mi

Which Western European country has only recently fully guaranteed a woman's right to vote in all local elections ?

a.

Switzerland. Though one of the world's most modern countries, universal suffrage was not complete until 1984.

Where is it common to burn fake money and other symbols of wealth to avoid harassment by ghosts?

121

a.

Chinese communities all over the world.

Freed American slaves returning to Africa founded what country ?

123

a.

Liberia — hence its name.

Which Latin American country has no standing army ?

125

a.

Costa Rica, with its constitution forbidding armed forces. In spite of, or because of this fact, Costa Rica is the only country in the region without a recent history of civil unrest or war.

The golden triangle, center of Asian opium production, is made up of parts of which countries ?

Myanmar, Laos and Thailand. Myanmar has also become a major methamphetamine producer with drug-dealing warlords controlling parts of the country.

*The people of which major world city have
little if any feeling of nationalism ?*

a.

Hong Kong. The city was for 99 years under British rule; then it was handed over to the Chinese. In neither situation did the people of Hong Kong have a reason to feel like a nation.

What region, not part of a country, is administered by way of a treaty with 42 signature countries ?

a.

Antarctica. The continent has been reserved for cooperative research.

Which country has the most executions ?

133

a.

China has the highest by far, over 5,000 annually. The government of China, however, will not provide statistics and the number is likely much higher. Of countries in which executions are counted, the USA, Iraq and Iran lead the world.

A giant comet hitting the earth is said to have caused the extinction of most life on earth including the dinosaurs. Where did it land ?

135

a.

Just north of the Yucatan peninsula in Southern Mexico. The event took place about 65 million years ago and accounts for the unique geography of the Yucatan.

*On which European peninsula are
no women permitted ?*

a.

The peninsula of Athos in Greece. With rules set by the local monasteries, the whole peninsula is off limits to females.

Q.

Which country had a government campaign to advise citizens that having two children, both daughters, is especially desirable ?

a.

Singapore. In the dominant Chinese culture boys have traditionally been preferable; the government was attempting to promote the value of girls.

Over 100 varieties of potatoes are in common use in what country ?

a.

Peru. Potatoes are a major
part of the diet for many
South American people.

Q.

Where is the world's largest seaweed harvesting area ?

a.

The California coast. Kelp is
a major California crop used
in hundreds of products
from lipstick to beer.

Q.

Where is it common in public for women to hold hands and men to hold hands or embrace, but a display of male/female affection is rare ?

a.

The practice may be most pronounced on the Indian subcontinent, but it is not uncommon in parts of the Middle East and North Africa.

*Where do people usually eat with a fork in one
hand and a spoon in the other?*

a.

Much of South East Asia.
Chopsticks are also
commonlpace, especially
for eating noodles.

Which U.S. state was once an independent country ?

a.

Texas. The Republic of Texas existed from 1836 to 1845.

RUSSIA

Anchorage

North Pacific Ocean

CANADA

Mackenzie

Peace

Great Lakes

Greenland (DENMARK)

Seattle

Missouri

Missouri

Ohio

New York

WASHINGTON, D.C.

The United States

Los Angeles

Houston

Miami

THE BAHAMAS

0   750   1500 km
0   750   1500 mi

Hawaiian Islands (U.S.)

MEXICO

Gulf of Mexico

CUBA

HAITI

DOM. REP.

GUATEMALA

JAM.

BELIZE

In which country is most of the population directly descended from the Mayans ?

**a.**

Guatemala. Its neighbors, such as Mexico, also have many Mayan descendents but not enough to form a majority of the population.

Which city has the least amount of space per person ?

a.

Macau. If all habitable land were divided equally, each person would have an area approximately the size of a ping-pong table.

Kurdish people live in Kurdistan, an area they would like to have acknowledged as an independent country. This region includes parts of which countries ?

a.

Parts of Turkey, Iran, Iraq,
Syria, and smaller portions
of Azerbaijan and Armenia.

The Spratly islands of the South China Sea are part of which country ?

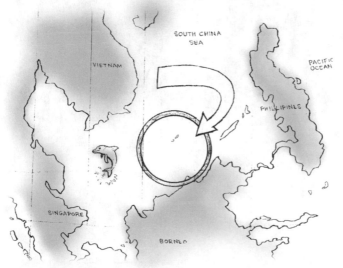

a.

China, the Philippines, Vietnam, Malaysia and Taiwan all claim them. The oil reserves make for bitter contention over their ownership.

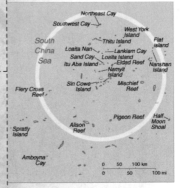

May Day, a holiday celebrated around the world to honor workers' rights and sometimes socialist ideology, originated where ?

159

a.

In Chicago, USA on May 1, 1886. At the time, the American Federation of Labor was pushing for an eight-hour workday and other basic rights for workers.

RUSSIA

Anchorage

Mackenzie

Greenland
(DENMARK)

CANADA

Peace

North
Pacific
Ocean

Seattle   Missouri

Great
Lakes

New York

Ohio

The United States

WASHINGTON, D.C.

Los Angeles

0   750   1500 km
0   750   1500 mi

Houston

MEXICO

Gulf
of
Mexico

Miami

THE
BAHAMAS

Hawaiian
Islands
(U.S.)

CUBA   HAITI
DOM. REP.

GUATEMALA   JAM.

BELIZE

*Nodding one's head up and down to gestures
"yes", and shaking right and left to indicate "no",
are common in many countries. But where
in Europe is "yes" gestured by dipping the head, and
"no" by raising up the head and eyebrows ?*

a.

In Greece.

Where does losing one's temper mean losing face ?

a.

In several countries, but Thailand may be the most strict. Losing one's temper is rare in public. Holding in one's frustration may come at a price, as the murder rate in Thailand is relatively high.

Q.

Where is the practice of casting a spell or hex on someone commonplace?

a.

In much of West Africa.
Employing a JuJu priest to
remove a hex is big business
in the region. Voodoo
originated in Benin but has
spread as far as the
Caribbean.

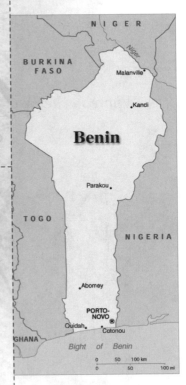

In which country does the law restrict the use of English language ?

167

a.

In Canada. In an effort to protect the French language, any English on public signs in Quebec must be accompanied by French in larger lettering.

A family's money is traditionally under the woman's control in what region?

a.

Various aboriginal communities worldwide and in much of East Asia. Some older generation Chinese men have limited access to the family's funds. In modern Japan, employers will often give secret bonuses to male employees to allow men to have some "play" money of their own.

Where may the kidnapping (and sometimes rape)
of a girl, act as a declaration of marriage ?

a.

"Zij poj niam" is practiced in Hmong areas of Laos. A man interested in a wife will go to her parents' house offering cigarettes and other tokens, and is usually given the girl. She is expected to weep and moan, even if she approves, while the groom is expected to ignore her protests.

Which country was founded mainly by former British prisoners and their offspring ?

a.

Australia. The island was once not only a British colony but a significant penal colony for the British Empire.

174

*What is the name of the new country formed
from part of Ethiopia ?*

a.

Eritrea, which gained independence in May, 1991.

Where was the first known case of AIDS found ?

a.

The Democratic Republic of the Congo. Blood taken from a man in 1959 who died of unknown causes in Kinshasa, was analyzed in 1998 and found to have the virus.

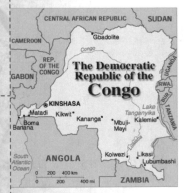

Which country has changed its name four times, finally settling on a name almost exactly the same as its neighbor's ?

a.

Formally Congo/Leopoldville, Congo/Kinshasa, the Belgian Congo and Zaire, it is now The Democratic Republic of the Congo. Its neighbor is the Republic of the Congo.

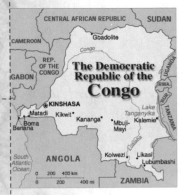

Which country manufactures the most baseballs ?

a.

Haiti has long supplied the world with baseballs.

Q.

Where did Charles Darwin find the most evidence for his theory of evolution ?

In the Galapagos Islands,
which offer a spectacular
array of unique wildlife.

Q.

Where is a competitive sport popular that involves pushing a canoe over a stretch of ice, then paddling through freezing water?

_a._

In Canada, with the
unusual sport of ice
canoeing.

Which U.S. state has the fewest snakes ?

a.

Hawaii. Historically there were no snakes on the Hawaiian Islands at all. Recently, sightings of imported snakes have caused alarm as they have no natural predators.

Q.

Caterpillars, bees, grasshoppers, maggots and spiders are found on the menu in which countries ?

a.

Insects are eaten worldwide. In Mexico, Irian Jaya, Venezuela, the Australian outback and other countries, they are consumed mostly by aboriginal peoples. But restaurants in Thailand and some gourmet establishments in Japan offer them as delicacies. Insects can be quite delicious.

Political Map of the World, April 2001

Which was the only country to have regular contact with Japan during its 200 years of isolation from the outside world, an isolation that ended only in the late 1800's ?

a.

Holland. For those not Dutch, landing on the island often meant death. Even shipwrecked sailors were executed with the intention of preventing any outside interference.

Which country makes the most movies per year ?

193

a.

India, in Bollywood with nearly 700 major movies a year.

*Which countries have the highest rate
of plastic surgery ?*

a.

Brazil and Venezuela, with
their very body-conscious
societies.

Q.

In which major city are dogs hanging from hooks a very common sight in front of restaurants ?

a.

Quangzhou (Canton), China. Dog is also considered food by some in Korea, Indonesia, Cambodia, Vietnam and parts of Africa.

198

Q.

*Which European country was moved
west at the end of World War II ?*

a.

Poland. Following the
liberation of Poland by the
USSR, Poland's west
border was moved into
Germany in compensation
for the USSR expanding
westward into Poland.

Which Latin American countries have their capital cities named after them ?

a.

Brazil, Panama, Guatemala and Mexico.

The people of Saigon, Vietnam usually refer to their city by what name ?

a.

Saigon. Though the official name is Ho Chi Minh City, Saigon remains the name of choice for locals.

Which country has a ratio of sheep to people of about 20 to 1 ?

a.

New Zealand. Its human
population is about 3.5
million, and it has more
than 70 million sheep.

*In what country does bottled water offered at gas
stations cost about three times
as much as the gasoline ?*

a.

The USA. Of the countries with similar, sometimes high-priced bottled water, most do not have the relatively low priced gasoline found in the USA.

The United States

Q.

Where is German commonly spoken in North America ?

a.

In Mennonite communities in northern Mexico.

210

Which Western European country has the lowest population growth in terms of births-per-person ?

a.

The Vatican, which is an independent country, followed by Italy.

212

Where are Islam's two holiest cites ?

a.

Mecca and Medina are both
in Saudi Arabia.

Which is the most visited city in the world ?

a.

Tijuana, Mexico. It is a major transit point for immigrants from all over Latin America heading to the USA, as well as a popular tourist destination for day-trippers from California.

Q.

What is the name of the island shared by Haiti and the Dominican Republic ?

217

a.

Hispaniola.

Q.

Dortmund, Germany; Tshingto, China; Tecata, Mexico: these cities have what beverage in common ?

a.

They are all cities that have
major brand beers named
after them.

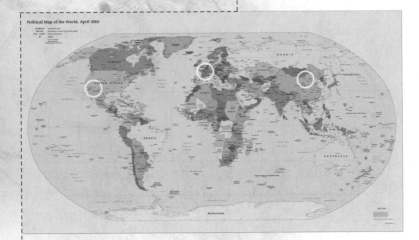

Political Map of the World, April 2001

Q.

Kwanzaa is a holiday celebrated by which African people ?

a.

African-Americans in the United States. Kwanzaa is a holiday to celebrate their cultural heritage and has a U.S. postal stamp to honor it.

The European space agency launches its Ariane rockets from which country ?

a.

From French Guiana in
South America.

From which island do lesbians get their name ?

a.

The Greek island of Lesbos.
Legend says only women
originally inhabited the
island.

In what countries besides Israel is the majority of the population Semitic ?

a.

In most of the Middle East and North Africa. Semitic refers to the ancient languages spoken in the region.

In which region is the cure for the common cold thought to be scraping the skin on one's neck with an oiled coin ?

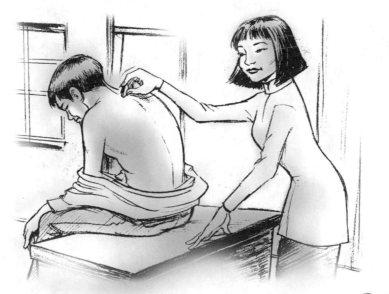

a.

In Vietnam. This very popular practice causes redness and discomfort, usually lasting a few days. Colds are thought to come from a bad wind, and the irritation is to provide a hole to let the wind back out.

Which countries have the lowest taxes ?

a.

Bahrain, Kuwait and Qatar. The oil-rich governments in some cases offer taxes in reverse: each citizen has the right to a variety of free services and governmental assistance.

Where is the undisputed belly dancing capital
of the world ?

a.

Cairo, Egypt.

Where is obesity considered a sign of beauty ?

a.

On several islands in the South Pacific and in parts of Nigeria. In many other developing countries, looking well-fed is a sign of affluence and prestige.

Political Map of the World, April 2001

Where were the Chinese fortune cookie and chop suey invented?

a.

In the USA. Chop suey comes from New York City's Chinatown and the fortune cookie from Los Angeles.

Which country is farthest from Los Angeles?

a.

The island of Mauritius
near Madagascar in the
Indian Ocean.

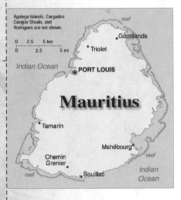

Agalega Islands, Cargados
Carajos Shoals, and
Rodrigues are not shown.

0   2.5   5 km
0   2.5   5 mi

Indian Ocean

★ PORT LOUIS

Goodlands

Triolet

Mauritius

Tamarin

Mahébourg

Chemin
Grenier

Souillac

reef

reef

reef

Indian
Ocean

Which country in the Middle East is only about 3% Arab ?

a.

Iran. It is: 51% Persian,
24% Azerbaijani, 8%
Gilaki and Mazandarani,
7% Kurd, 3% Arab,
2% Lur, 2% Baloch, and 2%
Turkmenand. In contrast,
Israel is about 17% Arab.

Q.

Political sex scandals have proved to get a candidate more votes rather than fewer in which democratic country ?

a.

France. In stark contrast, many politicians in the USA have seen their political lives unravel, when indiscretions are made public.

During the cold war, which European country was considered by the West to be a Soviet satellite but thought of by the USSR to be in the Western camp ?

245

a.

Yugoslavia. Though communist, it was one of only a few countries not to align itself with either superpower.

In which country is selling chewing gum against the law ?

a.

Singapore. In this attempt to reduce litter, Singapore has contributed to its image of having the most invasive laws of any industrialized country.

Where is it culturally unacceptable for a woman to wear close-fitting pants, but going topless is commonplace?

a.

In much of rural West Africa. The region is rich with cultural diversity, and so practices vary. The western fashion of pants on women is found only in the bigger cities.

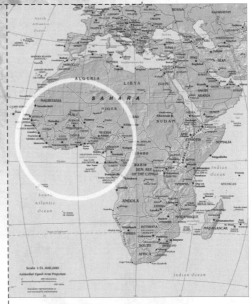

250

Where, when people die, are the bodies laid out for birds to eat ?

a.

In parts of India. Parsis believe that fire, earth and water are sacred, and burning or burying the corpse would be irreverent.

A Central American canal between the Atlantic and Pacific Oceans was first attempted in which country ?

Nicaragua. As early as 1567, King Philip II of Spain studied the idea. The connection of the San Juan River and giant Lake Nicaragua was tried and abandoned. More recent proposals have been rejected due to environmental concerns.

What country has the largest territorial possession which is neither geographically attached to the mainland of the country nor a commonwealth of it ?

a.

Denmark, with Greenland.
Greenland is independent
except for matters such as
foreign policy. The
"Greenlandic model" has
been of interest as a possible
solution in many parts of
the world where there are
minority conflicts between
former colonies and colonial
powers.

Where in Asia is reading a pornographic magazine in public not considered rude ?

a.

Japan. Promiscuity on the part of both men and women is also commonplace in the modern culture. This, too, is in sharp contrast to much of the rest of East Asia.

Soap is available at restaurant tables in which region ?

a.

Much of West Africa. Washing the right hand is usually done at the table with a bowl of water. A clean hand is important with the tradition of eating all food (even hot soup) with the fingers.

Where is the largest desert ?

a.

The entire continent of
Antarctica is considered a
desert. A desert is defined
by low precipitation not
temperature.

In what country is there no law against drunk driving ?

263

*a.*

In Iran. There are strict laws against alcohol but such beverages are widely available in the underground economy. Denying being inebriated will usually ensure avoiding punishment provided you are not caught actually possessing a container of alcohol.

Which country, about the size of Switzerland,

has the world's highest unclimbed peak,

*has normally only one airplane in the country
at any given time,*

*has a population living in large houses where
people eat lots of peppers and some beef and
pork -- although the religion prohibits killing
animals within the country,*

*has thousands of dogs allowed to bark all
night so they can scare off evil spirits,*

has millions of marijuana plants growing wild,

has no civil unrest or international enemies,

*has a national religion, which is a highly sexual
form of Buddhism, and*

*is a place where by law, almost everyone
wears a robe, the men often adding
argyle socks and dress shoes, while many elderly
people climb mountains barefoot?*

Bhutan. This remarkable country has been described as Shangri-La. Many who have been there feel that it has just about the most splendid natural environment and precious culture left on the planet.

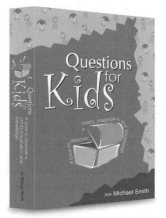

Questions for Kids

A Book to Discover a Child's
Imagination and Knowledge
By Michael Smith

Questions for Kids is a collection of 1,000 stimulating questions designed to inspire young minds. Even more than learning opportunities, these questions can serve as catalysts for thought-provoking family discussions. This book is a fun and educational resource for parents and children 5-8 years old.

Typical questions to read to children include:

- Can you buy anything with money?
- What would you do if you were scared of someone at school?
- What is the difference between a lake and an island?
- Does skin color make people smart or dumb?
- If you were a parent, would you punish a child if they made a bad mistake?

Genre: Parenting/Family Care/Children's: Education Resource/Game
ISBN: 0-9669437-1-6, Paperback, 5" x 7.25", 208 pages,

Publisher edition: $9.95

East West Discovery Press
P.O. Box 2393, Gardena, CA 90247.
Phone (310)532-1115 / Fax (310)768-8926

Note